MᶜLife

Selected Poems 1978-2004

by Richard Vargas

Deb —
Good luck —
Thanks for your
Support!
Richrd
Vrg

MAIN STREET RAG PUBLISHING COMPANY
CHARLOTTE, NORTH CAROLINA

Cover art by Devan A. Leonard of Albuquerque, NM.
Author photo on page 99 by Mark Bond.

Acknowledgments:

I would like to thank the editors of the following publications for
publishing these poems, sometimes in another version:

Blue Mesa Review, "friends"
Breakfast All Day, "McLife I," "tequila," "how it was"
Chelsea, "addicted," "going solo"
Chiron Review, "for an old teacher, an old friend (for Gerald
     Locklin)," "ancestor," "baby brother's blues"
Java Snob Review, "Walton's girls"
Main Street Rag, "5/16/02 8 months later," "4 eyes," "McLife III,"
     "Mars outside my window"
Rattle, "job interview," "California, here i go," "divorce me"
Rockford Register Star, "waiting in line at Logli's"
Rockford Review, "sex ed," "the Jesus i want to know"
Touched by Eros, "altar... for Kathy"
Willow Review, "Okla. bombing remains to be buried..."
Wormwood Review, "workweek," "dying; a vision,"
     "dying; a vision #2," "race war"

Library of Congress Control Number: 2005933353

ISBN 1-930907-94-X

Produced in the United States of America

Main Street Rag Publishing Company
4416 Shea Lane
Charlotte, NC 28227
www.MainStreetRag.com

Special thanks to:

Marvin Malone, Edward Field, Gerald Locklin, Diane Wakoski, Luis J. Rodriguez, Nila Northsun, Virgil Suarez, and Linda Roth.

This collection is dedicated to the memory of my brother, Robert... the best there ever was.

Contents

FOREWORD

by Edward Field

Richard Vargas is unique among my poet correspondents—rather than hit the Delete button after reading the poems he e-mails me, I save all of his.

Now, after reading this book, demonstrating his devastating charm, his versatility and his vital subject matter, this is my chance to say that I totally approve of his poems, and wish everybody could read them. Why aren't they in national magazines, read on the radio, on the Op-Ed page of the New York Times? At least. With this publication I can't see how they can be overlooked. I foresee much attention, many readers.

Ricardo and I have a couple of basic things in common: He's ethnic like me, which gives you a major advantage—it sets you just enough apart in this country to clearly observe and distinguish the shit from the shinola. Though I could never get through college as he did, we both spent a stretch in the military, and made it to lieutenant—for poor boys we've got a right to be proud of that. Also, of course, we're both on the poetry track, and are late developers—we had a lot of life's hard lessons to learn, and poetry was a useful tool there. And the struggles to survive turned out good for the poetry. And yes, Richard, getting that book published changed my life! As this book should change yours.

What's more, like me he puts the raw material of his life into his poems, as this book demonstrates—what else is there for a serious person to write about? Perhaps it's our "colorful" background, but I personally believe in telling all, though this is often scorned as "mere" confessional poetry. Bullshit. Poetry speaks to others when the soul and body are bared. Richard certainly does that, bares his heart and his…everything. I must say, his sex poems are the most convincing argument for heterosexuality I've seen—he tells how he became conscious of this…propensity…at the age of four! At the same time his poetry respects us others in all our horny diversity. Though when I read his family poems I know we're all alike. And politically? His anti-war poems are absolutely the best, the most trenchant and moving I've seen and I forward them to friends who are also dismayed by what we are doing in the Middle East. From his computer to George Bush's ear. Please God! Save the planet!

The Establishment encourages poetry to be religious, esoteric, tame—because poetry unleashed is a revolutionary form and is threatening. But Richard Vargas's poems defy such limits that mostly make poetry, even if technically brilliant, boring to anyone but specialists. He is part of a poetic revolution emanating from Long Beach, California, sparked by the remarkable Gerry Locklin, encouraging poetry to be about issues we all care about, both public and private. As Richard demonstrates, these poems work as public performance or read to yourself—they're gripping both ways. His supple language, language we can all understand, says exactly what he wants to say, and this poet says LIVE! Best of all we can hear his voice saying it—and with his generosity of spirit and his openheartedness, I imagine all his new readers will fall in love with him as I have. Once you start this book you'll read every poem from the beginning to the end.

MᶜLIFE

drive-in baby

no one ever told me
but i always knew

under a starry spring night
while the smell of popcorn
lingered in the cool California air
like a cheap dime store perfume
the tinny sound of a
drive-in speaker serenaded
two horny teenagers driven
by the rising fever between
their legs

these are my parents
hiding behind the steamed windshield
my young father fumbling
with the reluctant bra snap
my mother's skirt
creeping up inch by inch
to the point of no return
their Saturday night kisses
tasting of spearmint gum
and coke

these are my parents
laying down in the backseat
with just enough knowledge
to know where to put what
because there was no sex ed
for them unless you count
Lauren Bacall standing in the doorway
looking back at the camera and
giving those famous instructions
"you do know how to whistle, don't you?
...just put your lips together and blow."

these are my parents
her head bumping against
the door handle
while he gets a cramp in his leg
but both beyond knowing
the difference between pain
and pleasure
as the springs of the backseat
sang in unison with all the other springs
at the Compton drive-in
squeak...squeak...
squeak...squeak...
squeaksqueaksqueak
squeaksqueak

until they all stopped at once

these are my parents
holding each other tight
believing this is all there is
all there needs to be
their dreams wrapped around
Hollywood fantasies and
a rock n' roll soundtrack

these are my parents
and that's how
they brought me
into this world

sex ed

by the age of six
i knew i wanted to
marry Donna Reed's daughter
with a Marilyn Monroe
on the side

no masa making
tortilla rolling
bean boiling
sweat-dripping-down-
her-forehead mamacita
for me

i wanted prissy
starched skirts
clean unblemished skin
under furry pink
cashmere sweaters
or
a curvy long
legged blonde
pouting full red lips
while cool air shoots up
her steamy summer dress

now i dream
and Marilyn does
lap dances at the Surf Lounge
for ten bucks
tells me to keep my hands
to myself

Donna's little girl serves
me meat loaf again and again
yells at me for drinking too
much beer

says she should have
listened to her mother

we film before
a live audience
of abuelitas mamas
hermanas tias
their silence is louder
than any
canned laugh

jobs

in the beginning we like to think
they're temporary
just something to pass
the time until we get the break
we're all looking for
pay off some bills
stash some cash in the bank
maybe buy a new car

we get tired of it
sooner or later
but we stick it out
it isn't that hard
why look a gift horse
in the mouth
it could be worse
so we stick it out
learn how to say yes
when we really mean no
live a routine paced by
the punching of timeclocks
the cashing of paychecks
yeah, we stick it out

but we feel differently on
that warm and beautiful
spring morning
when we wake up
stare at the ceiling
feel like a neurotic hamster
whose life has become
a neverending series
of 40 hour treadmills

separated only by weekends
that get dangerously shorter
all the time

it's a living

it's called customer service
trying to help my fellow man
make sense of the medical insurance
some slick carpetbagging agent
talked him into buying

there are no easy answers
like today
the guy on the phone
was speaking with restraint
holding on to his dignity
but i know begging when i hear it
his voice cracked as he told me
the doctor tending to his dying wife
was getting phone calls from one
of our case managers
being pressured to get her
released from the hospital

please he said
please ask them to stop
she's in so much pain
my wife my best friend
she's in a lot of pain and
there's nothing they can do
please stop the phone calls

i tell him he's got us mixed up
with someone else
there is no record
of any phone calls
in his wife's file
but i know better

i want to put him on hold
go find the sterile room with
white walls where faceless people
hold jelly donuts gripped
tight in their pudgy hands
as they put dollar signs
on the way we die

i want to stick my head inside
remind them that
sooner or later we all
finish the race
sometimes it ain't too pretty
but in the end
if we're lucky
we'll have the love
of a precious few
maybe the ability to stare
death in the eye
so let this one go
just leave her be

but instead i assure
the guy i'll do my best
to find out what's going on
wait for him to hang up
decide to take my break
10 minutes early

times like this i wish
i'd taken up smoking

job interview

it's been 4 yrs since my last one
so my gut was queasy
as i sat there in the lobby
wearing my navy blue blazer
trying to look serious and
job worthy
when this baby face
showed up
introduced himself
shook my hand
took me to a room
where a young woman
joined us and i was thinking
both of them are old
enough to be my kids
if i had any

so
since i was being interviewed
by the Mickey Mouse club
and i had more work
experience than the two
of them put together
any semblance of being
nervous went out the window
my answers were well
thought out as i took
their questions like fastballs
which i easily hit out of
the ballpark

then the girl, er, woman
asked me which would
i rather be: a hummingbird
or a woodpecker?
we all laughed but then i

realized they actually wanted
an answer and i was thinking
what's next? would i rather
be a dung beetle or a wart
on a fat guy's butt?
a piece of cheese
or a brand new
Penthouse magazine in a
men's prison?
i began to think of all
the possibilities when
baby face cleared his throat
letting me know they were
waiting for my answer

my first thought was i'd rather
peck than hum and since
i too have a pecker and
frequent woodies one could
say my choice should be obvious

but i knew that wasn't what
they wanted to hear
they had pens in hand
ready to write down
my answer
and all i could think about
was getting the
hell outta there alive

and how good a
cold beer would taste
right about then

laid off

they hold their heads high
say they saw it coming
(they did) and knew
how to take it in stride
(they didn't)
all week whispered conversations
about unemployment benefits
and maybe going back to school
then the planning out loud for all to hear
about meeting at a local bar Friday after work
to get blasted and let it all hang out

if you were one of the lucky ones
you'll pass because after the 3rd round
weird looks will begin to come your way
the comic book bubbles over their
heads where you can read their thoughts
will say the same thing:
"why not him?"

then you'll blink an eye and see it
reflected back at you in their faces
the shotgun someone will clean tomorrow
and come Monday you're sitting at your
desk taking a phone call
whipping around to see what made
the loud metallic click behind you

you'll blink again
now you're back in the bar
Hank Williams is on the jukebox
they're all lifting their glasses
in your direction

you read someone's lips
as he/she says:
"watch out man,
you could be next."

piss test

dick in hand
plastic cup in
the other
waiting for
something to happen
the faucets on the
sink are gone
the drain is plugged
the window is locked
a sign on the wall
says don't flush

your bladder
relaxes
you pee the
required
amount
realize you
hold your innocence
in your hand
wonder how
it has come
to this

workweek

Mondays, i approach my job with the attitude
of an offensive guard. only i can truly appreciate
what i have to do. i don't want the glory,
only recognition of the fact that i'm there.

on Tuesdays, i feel more sure of myself than the day
before, but like the defensive tackle, i hold my ground,
don't take any chances. it only takes a cleverly
disguised draw play to keep me honest.

Wednesdays will find me cradling the ball
as i attempt to go wide, stutter-stepping all the way,
looking for that moment of hesitation created by
a good head fake. then, darting through the line,
dodging arms and shoulders like a scared rabbit
zigzagging between the trees. and even though i hear
footsteps, i can never look over my shoulder, knowing
the moment i begin to do so my game will never
be the same.

Thursdays are do or die. like the wide receiver
running that dreaded pattern over the middle,
at the mercy of sadistic linebackers and defensive backs,
i wonder why i do it. leaping into the air with antelope
grace and abandon, i prepare myself for the blow that
will leave my head ringing for the rest of the day,
my body wracked with suicidal pain. but if i'm lucky,
i'll catch 'em with their thumbs up their asses, and
before they can disengage 'em, i'll race past, make a
first down, keep the drive alive.

on Fridays, like the polished quarterback, i've got my
ground game established, allowing me to fill the stadium
air with beautiful, spiraling bombs that descend with an
accuracy that would have given even Hitler a hard on.

i'm looking good, really good.
and slowly i begin to realize why somebody
created this crazy game.

for an old teacher, an old friend
(for Gerald Locklin)

dear Gerry,
so how's it going?
it's been awhile
i hope you sometimes kick back
in your faculty office and wonder
what the hell ever became of me
i kinda dropped out of sight
after my episode in the Long Beach
drunk tank in '79, maybe it scared me off,
but things weren't the same after that
i like to think you knew i'd be back
because after all, i'd tasted good poetry
felt it pour out from my fingertips
and once we're marked by the beast
embrace it...we're doomed for the duration
i remember our attempt to comprehend *Finnegan's Wake*
(you wanted to read the book, but kept putting it off
so you figured if you taught the class you'd
have to pick it up)
the joy i had getting drunk before noon
and, together, trying to decipher Joyce
at his best was a highlight of my education
or the time i started publishing my poetry mag
and the lead poem was something you wrote
called "i wish they could all be California girls"
the subject matter having to do with fellatio
and the local bronzed babes
the first printer i went to was so disgusted
he refused to accept my order, called my
little mag "filth" and "dirty"
the last time i saw you was in '84
returning to So. California i found myself
asked to give a reading at an art gallery
in Belmont Shore...i was pleased to know
someone still appreciated my work, but Magic

was leading the Lakers against the Boston Celtics
that night, so i agreed to appear with mixed emotions
i knew i had made the wrong decision when
halfway through my set i looked up and saw
some idiot slumped in his chair, sound asleep

then i realized the whole crowd consisted
of wannabes waiting for me to shut up
so they could read their stuff
i wrapped things up early and walked out
with a bad taste in my mouth
found a bar and caught the 2nd half of what
turned out to be a great game
but as i exited i walked right past you
didn't even extend my hand

which brings me to last night
a bunch of us were sharing a few pitchers
at Cannova's
i stumbled to the john
and when i looked in the mirror
it struck me
there i was in my k-mart polo shirt
my baggy khaki pants
my "comfortable" shoes
(and after being out of California for a year
and for once not caring about how i look)
my love handles were blending into
my soft, 41 year old belly
top all this off by my piss poor
attempt at growing facial hair
and the only thing missing are your trademark
Clark Kent glasses
but the kicker was the pee stain between my legs
cause i'd whipped my pecker in too fast

"my God" i said,
"it's him. i'm turning into Gerry."

i can only hope this reads like the compliment
it's supposed to be
and the poetry keeps flowing
for both of us
always...the Kid

the Jesus i want to know

no, it's not the one kneeling
in the garden asking the Old Man
for a break just before the local
thugs surrounded Him and said
"you in a heap of trouble, boy..."

and even though i enjoy a drop
of the grape with the best of them
i'd have to decline the wedding
where He pulled off the ultimate
trick and kept turning water
into wine
earning Him the moniker
Party Animal of Nazareth

without a doubt
the Jesus i want to know
is the one who lost it
went berserk on the moneychangers
at the temple picked up a switch
brought it down left and right
leaving stinging red welts on
their eel-like skin
the sound of coins landing on
the hard ground
tables crashing over domino style

at that moment did He hear the moans
of a host of angels?
did fear grip His mortal heart?

i like to think
He caressed the violent gene
imbedded deep in the flesh
embraced the purity of our
rise and fall

Sodom and Gomorrah revisited

it's not like i've learned any lessons
keep making the same mistakes over and over
the occasional slap on the wrist is just
what it says
i go to the well
of syrupy sin
time and time again
keep getting away with it
screw the gods screw the planet screw myself
until like Dr. Frankenstein
realizing a bad experiment has gone worse
someone pulls the plug

but this is what i know
all i am
and when told not to look back
i, too, will sneak one last peek
at the life i am leaving

welcome the taste of salt on my lips
marvel at sand bleached white
reflecting the final fiery
flash of light

dying; a vision

i am sitting at the bar inside a dark tavern.
it is raining outside, and the only thing
i have in common with this strange land
is an appreciation for a cold beer on a wet day.
the bartender is at the far end of the bar
talking with a group of men in a language
i don't understand. they look at me and begin
to laugh.
pretending not to notice, i gesture with my
empty bottle. the bartender ignores me.
"i'd like another, please."
still no response.
(in Singapore i had encountered the same problem,
only to find out that i could handle five men at
the same time and still walk away in less than
three pieces.)
i throw the bottle, smashing the mirror behind the bar,
saying "fuck you" in a language everyone understands.
then, making a quick head count, i remember the time
i had my fortune told by a moustached woman who had
gold teeth. "twelve," she had said, "is your unlucky
number."
as two of the men block off the door,
the rest engage in the familiar shattering of glass,
letting me know what to expect;
they surround me, the jagged edges of beer bottles
like the teeth of so many piranhas.

dying; a vision...#2

my mother was talking to him.
it was important, i could tell
by the tone of her voice.
but he never looked up from
the squat-like stance he used
when watering the front yard
on warm summer nights.

he just stared at the spray of water,
which looked like a smashed
mirror hanging, suspended in mid-air,
reflecting the lights of night
back into his face.

for my father

heroin
enters my blood
streams down the
breaks down
heroin the liver
better than a lover
teases my limbic pleasures
triggers my sinful treasures
reassures my medulla
oh so oblongata
heroin strokes
purrs like the fat cat
drowsiness when
the heroin comes in

heroin my life
better than a wife
brings my breathing
down low
slows it
controls it
bass of brain
surrenders
thump thump
to sweet sweet
heroin feels so good

causes carbon
dioxide backup
like an L.A. freeway
at 6 p.m. on a Friday
when it is Payday
and heroin awaits

coma
heroin coma
up ahead

the man at the end of
the ramp awaits
the bedazzled lamb
heroin the sweet butcher
fills my lungs with
fluids
drowns me
smiling
a root beer froth
covers the mouth
rooty toot toot
hmmmm heroin

the heart still beats
but the heroin takes the
breath away like
the consummate lover
turns pupils into fading
pinpoints of pleasure

till i am led
to the bed
where the brain
is laid down
laid
down
dead

and
the hero in
my dream laughs
pulls me close
kisses me deep
slips me the tongue
welcomes me to
the world
i can never
leave

watering the grass

getting home from your ten hour
shift as an apprentice welder
you would grab a cold beer
turn on the water
and hose in hand stand in the fading light
of the summer day

with our mother by your side you would talk
about the affairs of the day
pick up the football and toss me a few
my siblings would run about the yard
vying for your attention and we all basked
in the warmth of what would someday be labeled
a Hallmark moment
then, you would bend your knees and squat
bring the spray close to the ground
move it from side to side like a metronome
set to the rhythm of your thick blue collar wrist
it was then that you became lost in the act
keeping your thoughts to yourself
so that even your wife left you alone
herding us into the house
a mother hen gathering her chicks

you kept the grass lush and thriving
even during the dog days of August
and now i am trying to do the same
but my lawn is brown and yellow
when i walk on it
it makes a crunchy noise like shredded wheat
my water bill is going to be sky high
i'm ready to throw in the towel
but then i recall the irony of all this
how you devoted yourself to keeping something alive
while pushing a needle into your arm
sucking out your life bit by bit

i know it's hopeless, doesn't make sense
but this is my tribute
when i squat, my thoughts do not
turn to you, but of how sweet candy skulls
taste on the Day of the Dead
and the universal sounds made by the dying
when gasping for air...
the sigh, the gentle spasms,
the release

friends

they started showing up
at our door a few weeks
after he died
stopping by after work
hanging around for hours
like junkyard dogs waiting
for a bitch to go into heat
all wanting to take their turn first

i watched them play with my little brother
toss him into the air until he was
tired and lost interest
my sisters would drift off
to their room
play Barbie and Ken
but i stayed put
staring at the black and white screen
taking in every word
watched from the corner
of my eye as they waited
for her to turn her back
get them a soda or ice tea
her antelope grace putting a
grin on their faces
like hyenas moving in for the kill

she never gave in
always sent them home with
their dick in hand
headed out the door
they would look at me
shake a finger
say "you better be good
mind your mom or else"

i would stand there
my father's presence
in my 10 yr. old fist
trembling

addicted

it's in my genes
they have been on both sides of my family tree
men who swap it all for that little prick
in the arm, the warm rush flowing through
their cold veins as they walk the streets
like Hollywood extras out of a cheap zombie flick

so it was only a matter of time
my poison being more accessible, right off the grocery shelf
i take a daily fix, sometimes two
like it best with egg salad or tuna
slather both sides of bread with the off-white goo
then the sandwich fixings so thick
it squirts out on all sides when i take a bite
i tried to stop, imagined i was eating a mechanic's rag
dropped in a bucket of oil
but it still tasted so good
in desperation i bought a jar of the "no-fat" crap
but my taste buds have been warped
and as for going cold turkey...
well, let's just say the frigid old broad
didn't know what the hell she was talking about
when she said "just say no"

sometimes i think i can feel it clinging to the walls
of my arteries, wonder when the stuff is going to kill me
but it taste so good   i love it   gotta have it
daddy, daddy
i know now
know where you were coming from
it was never about being hard to stop

but how easy
it is getting started

ancestor

word has it he crossed the river
at El Paso when the streets were still dirt
when a mexican had to step aside to let
a white man pass
he planted his seed here
started a whole branch of the family tree
and then he killed a man
(i don't know why or how
but i'm sure money and a woman were involved
also several shots of tequila
and an old pistola from the revolution)
the sheriff got word to him
he was good as dead if he got caught
so he crossed the river back
to Mexico...the mother of our people

and word has it he crossed back
several times to visit his family
once he had to spend all day
in the out house while the sheriff's men
searched the place
terrorized his wife and children
but he always got away
like the fox he truly was

some would say it is a shame
to have a killer's blood in my veins
and worse, to be proud of it
but i think back to the times
i refused to be fucked with
convinced guys bigger than me to back off
knowing if my bluff was called
i would be history
maybe they could see the old man's craziness
in my eyes...the button they dare not push

it's a good thing to have some bad blood
it's a good thing

abuelo's curse

didn't want much
his secret for always picking out
the juiciest and sweetest watermelon
how to pound a nail straight
and true with one mighty swing
of the hammer
his fighting cock strut
but he pretty much ignored me
the fat little kid who liked
dinosaurs and hated baseball

until my thirteenth year
discovered i could hear lies
before lips moved
sweet nothings dripped down
my tongue like maple syrup
from a fresh cut in the tree

while classmates worried
about a new crop of zits
the day before the sock hop
i heard ugly truths on
far away winds
wrote them down
called them poems

learned to pick up a word
turn it over and over in my hands
sniff thump squeeze
just knew it was ready

could nail an enemy to the wall
spit sharp pieces of iron
pound them with my bare fist

now i walk through this life
a barnyard rooster with
pico de gallo kisses on my lips

and Adolfo
mi abuelo
my macho horny bastard
grandpa shaman
stares back at me from the mirror
bearing gifts

his cupped hands holding
his greatest strengths
in a nest made of
all his weaknesses

abuelita

how hard it must have been
not to be able to communicate with me
in my language, and my refusal to learn yours
how could i hear your stories?
how you loved the feel of books and the magical places
they could send you but in the third grade you
were taken out of school because your family had found
land to farm that was too far from town
and an educated woman had no worth in your culture
how you loved to dance, went to all the fiestas
and your poor brothers always ended up in fights
with the barnyard cocks who strutted too close for their liking
how you married a man out of resignation, saying "yes"
when you realized how limited your choices were
popping out babies with ease while your husband started chasing
freshly pressed dresses and the women who wore them
how you watched your children grow up with calluses
on their tiny hands
suffer from heat induced nose bleeds
as the family picked crops from Tejas to California
how their father bought a house for them to live in
then left you, moved on to a fresh start
how you fought the good fight and lost
as your sons became addicted to the dreams
they injected into their arms
how you succumbed to the asthma, retreated to your room
surrounded yourself with statues of baby Jesus, the Blessed Virgin,
and your favorite, St. Anthony...the votive candles would flicker
through the night, casting shadows of the holy across the walls
of the room (when you were asleep i would sneak in, pretend i
was watching a puppet show, and wait for the angels to come)
finally, how death laid an egg in your bowels
then made you wait for your name to be called out
in the black velvet pain of your longest night

my most vivid memory:
i am four or five, sitting next to you
on your bed, when you begin to unravel
the long silver braid touching the small
of your back
it smelled sweet like clean sheets
that had just been slept in
you smiled at me with your indian face
as you brushed and your hair looked like the
shiny plumage of a sacred bird
as you gently wrapped your arms around my tiny body
flew me to the moon
and back

we never

made love in the light
and although it's been over thirty years
i can recall the action like it was yesterday
the soft moan and twitch as
i would press my lips to the ones between
your legs, wondering how you always
managed to smell so clean
as i worked my way up to your flat belly
hard from your daily workouts
on the high school drill team
your firm white breasts with a
soft glow all their own, nipples
pink and erect beckoning for my kiss

you would offer your soft neck to me
turning your head slightly to the side
in a gesture of gentle surrender
as our tongues found one another
all slippery warm and wet
i would wonder at the strength of your
seventeen year old thighs creating a vise-like
grip around my varsity football hips
then, joined at the groin i would raise
myself up, breaking the body seal
created by our sensual sweat
there between my arms i could make out
the outline of your nose, eyes, and mouth
your long blond hair always fell
just right, creating a golden aura circling your
head and resting on your shoulders

this is why i don't read the bible
because when it tells the story of
the guy who wrestled all night with one
of God's angels
i can't believe they cut this part out

Wolfman

i was at that age where i
was too young to drive, drink, or get laid
but i knew i wanted those things real bad
so weekends i would go to bed
put the big transistor radio under my pillow
listen to it while waiting for the sleep of the restless
my stepfather had told me not to do this anymore
so the act had some significance
then one night while searching for a decent station
i heard his voice, it sounded like someone with a
piece of sandpaper stuck in his throat
he was harassing some tight ass phone operator
asking her to "whiz" on him
he played my anthem, the Who's version of Summertime Blues
then threw in some Otis Redding and Cloud Nine
by the Temptations
i stayed with him throughout the night, his selection of music
defining the anguish between my ears and burning in my groin
listeners from all over the country called in to proclaim
their love for him, and that long hot summer
when i walked the razor blade edge of teenage insanity
spent hours staring at the blank walls in my room
had romantic interludes with mary palm and
her five sisters with greater and greater frequency
i can honestly say he saved my life

you're gone now
i'm at the age when the people who left their mark on me
are passing on
but thanks to you, Wolfman
it's 1970, i'm climbing the walls
XERB is on the radio
and you're every telephone operator's worst nightmare
every zit faced adolescent's best friend

leading us in unison as we sneak outside at 2 a.m.
climb the roofs of our parent's houses
look up to the black void above

howl at a moon we can see
but can't touch

Woodstock

lifted my copy at Zodys
blended into a background
of imported electric appliances
and cheap underwear
casually checked out the
entries and exits
of the record dept
before making my move

i was there to take back
what the self-appointed
moneychangers of my
teen religion were
trying to sell me

bold and stupid
i hid my prize behind
another package
carried under my arm
walked passed the old guy
in his gray security uniform
waved as i went out the door

once i got home
closed the door to my room
pulled down the shades
turned up my
Montgomery Ward stereo
full blast

Jimi's guitar made the sounds of
artillery rounds exploding
in my brain

my war had begun
it was going to be a long one

why i can't play basketball anymore

i was shooting baskets in the driveway
faking and slicing between the team i hated the most
the Celtics never had a chance on my home court
i knew every crack in the cement
where the surface went from rough to smooth
and how tennis shoes would skid an extra
two inches when stopping on a dime
from which angle i had to attack the basket without
slamming into the garage door like a pancake
my hoop was crooked too, giving me another edge
since only i knew where the rebounds would be
i always won, and while calling the game on the radio
Chick Hearn would praise my ability to put
my opponent "in the popcorn machine"
as the crowd gave me a standing ovation

on this day my stepfather interrupted the game
had to be somewhere in a hurry
i stepped aside while he backed the car out of the garage
it was always a tight squeeze, but if i sucked in my
stomach and pressed my backside into the fence
he could glide by me with a couple of inches to spare
but this time he braked when i was beside the driver's window
and as i stood there, unable to move in any direction
feeling truly trapped by a tenacious full court press
he started talking yard work, something about mowing the lawn
it was on my agenda, and as i tried to explain
he reached out the window and grabbed my crotch
it took everything i had to suppress the whimper trying to escape
through my clenched jaw
then, he let go
didn't say a word
vanished into the street

i stood there, puzzled
waited for the ref to call a foul
but when the whistle didn't blow
i looked up through blurred tears

knew i was alone
under a cloudless sky

photograph

it clings to the dark walls
of my mind
one of those ancient
cave paintings imprinted
on stone somewhere
in Europe

a photo of my sisters
and a family friend taken
when they were kids
three girls approaching
that inevitable decision:
Barbie or boys?

wearing shorts and summer
tops in the California sun
posing in the backyard
at some family BBQ

in the background is
the house on Pennsylvania St
yellow stucco with
pea green trim

the tree stump to the right
belongs to a perfectly good
apricot tree we cut down
because its rotting fruit
drew too many flies

behind them is the
window to my sisters'
bedroom with the
shade pulled down

and everytime i
think about this
photo i remember
years later as
adults one of
my sisters telling
me how five minutes
before posing she was
on the other side of
that window with our stepfather
how he had his
hands all over her
on her
in her

now i'm destined
to always look
for the picture
within the picture
wince when family
albums are passed
around

not because of
the memories inside

but the ones left out

baby brother's blues

he was just a kid who loved to tease
our sisters and counted on me to keep
the neighborhood bullies at bay
but our stepfather did not like him as he was
right away he tightened the screws
shaved his head
slapped him around
played mind games with him
like waking him up at two in the morning
and making him shine his shoes
he was only seven or eight
the time he took him to downtown L.A.
made him get on the floor of the car
so he could not see where they were going
then he was told to sit up and before he
could ask about the tall buildings and all the people
scurrying about like ants the old man opened the door
kicked him out on the sidewalk
drove off without saying a word
years later my brother would say he had never been so scared
cried as he realized he had been dumped
on the street like an unwanted pet, until
our stepfather circled the block
laughed as he picked him up like
it was a big joke

his childhood became a thing to endure
losing a piece of himself with every blow
to his head, carrying what was left of his psyche
in the palm of his hand
like pieces of precious glass

last year i drove up to see him
surrounded by cold stone walls
and fences with razor sharp edges
men with loaded guns watched from above

as we hugged and talked
this is how i remember my baby brother

in Folsom blue

trying to fill the holes in his soul
with Camel cigarettes
and crude tattoos

going solo

i practice religiously
always prepared for those
times when i'm by myself
falling asleep waking up
only to wrap my arms around
stale air and nothing else
while the loneliness of the
times i live in cut my insides
like a dull knife

this is when i give in
surrender to my own touch
feel fingertips sending sensations
from synapse to synapse
my body becomes a static
wave of electrical sparks
me a flashing neon sign suspended
over Times Square
my mood determines the style
sometimes quick and powerful
the almost brutal force lifting my
hips off the bed
surging upward into space
or i can pace myself
with the patience of boiling liquid
cresting the rim, receding, cresting
receding until the final overflow
pleasure ripples from the tips
of my hair down to toes
flexed and rigid

some say God calls me a sinner
a man without self control
i say He knew what he was doing
could see ahead to those times

those humid summer nights
simmering in my personal
solitary hell
when the time it takes
a bead of sweat to slide
down the bridge of my nose
seems like an eternity
and my closest friends might as
well be the stars in the sky

McLife I

he was old
shuffled his feet
to a much slower drum
than the rest of us
looked almost comical
in his teal blue polo shirt
with the trademark golden arches
embroidered on his chest
the baseball cap suited for
pimple faced teenagers was
too big, rested on his ears
and tilted to one side
as he bussed the tables
left littered by single moms
and their undisciplined brats

i was going to say something
like "yo, pops, shouldn't you
be out casting a few on a nice
day like this?" but the look
in his eyes said "don't"
letting me know he had
been let go before his time
screwed out of his pension
while heartless young men
in expensive suits exercised
stock options, downsized for profit
vacationed in Cancun
and pulled his medical insurance
like a rug from under his feet

now, snot nosed kids
who think FDR is a new rap group
shoot him orders, hand him a mop
tonight he will go home
watch reruns of the Honeymooners

drink Jack Daniels from a pint
dream of winters in Phoenix
and the trigger he's
lost the nerve to pull

tequila

drinking it straight
is kinda like climbing
into the ring with
a real pro
one of those mexican
fighters with a record
of 40 wins by knockout
and two losses by TKO
so the first shot goes
down like liquid fire
but man you
know you're alive
dancing and juking
keeping a safe distance
scoring with jabs
and uppercuts at will
it feels soooo good
you order another
more fire in the gut
forget the lemon and salt
you ain't no sissy
your opponent has a trickle
of blood squirting
from the corner of his eye
the black man
with the silver head of hair
sticking straight up
sitting at ringside is smiling
his toothy grin blinding you
with that timeless flash
of polished gold
hell you say
this is soooo easy
another please and this shot
is smooth   the fire now
more like a hot kiss

the young woman on the barstool
next to you
is impressed and squeezes your knee
the mexican boxer begins
to wear down
his breathing telling you
his heart is going to explode
any minute
he's yours for the taking
you order another and another
admiring the amazons
strutting around the ring
holding up the posters
announcing what round it is
knowing you can have
your pick or maybe
all of them later
then sensing it's time
to finish him off
you decide to go in
for the kill
and suddenly he switches
his stance
you were fighting
a right hander
but now he's a lefty
you walking into
a head shot that lowers
your jaw to the bar
your back to the ropes
he begins to jab
hot pokers of leather
into your ribs
tenderizing you like
one big piece of meat

and while lowering your
arms to protect the body
you hear your date ask
from far far away
"can you still drive..."
feel her hands in your
pockets searching for
the keys as tequila
grins back at you
with scheming
conquistador eyes

nature poem... for Amy

sitting in the living room on a lazy Sunday
watching NFL playoffs and getting drunk
on mimosas
starting on our third bottle of cheap champagne
we know we're getting deep
when she says the other day she saw
a most peculiar thing
a squirrel scrambled up a tree
with a piece of bread only to be
cornered by a couple of crows
trying to snatch his lunch
when, she says, the squirrel tore
off a chunk of bread and dropped
it to the ground
the crows followed it down
fought amongst themselves
while he ate the rest at his leisure
she talks about how she's never
seen that on any nature show and i say
yeah, but you probably didn't see
the squirrel wipe his defiant
ass with the bread
before he gave it up
a true mammalian response, i say,
illustrating why we rule over birds who
still think like the little dinosaurs
that they are
but, she says, crows eat roadkill
and have been known to eat
a stinky furry ass from time to time
so they really weren't bothered
sooner or later that ass belongs to them
anyway, which, if you think about it
kinda makes them the republicans
of the animal kingdom

i pop the cork
realize why drunk english majors
don't write for the Discovery channel

throwing up at Grandma's

you never know when
you'll fill the void
find a best friend
where there are none
like the time Dan Swanson
and i were eating a 1 a.m.
breakfast at Grandma's
in Loves Park
he ordered an omelet
i got my usual corned beef hash
three eggs over easy
our waitress was good
had a hard face
like she'd been through
tough times
but she kept the coffee
topped off and fresh
she knew what mattered

so while she was stopping by
to check up on us
i began to feel queasy
a bitter taste creeping
up my esophagus
erupting molten lava
dribbled out the corner
of my mouth
to her credit
the waitress just stood there
studying the pool of
pink puke on the yellowed
linoleum as if she could
tell my fortune by
staring at it long enough

i got up and walked
to the restroom
rinsed out my mouth
in the sink
went back to my table
where the hostess
the waitress and
a busboy gathered around
my puddle of vomit
trying to decide
who was gonna clean it up
i took the rag from the hostess
wiped it up myself
gave the waitress a five dollar bill
swore on the graves of my ancestors
i wasn't drunk
well, not that drunk

finally sitting down
to continue where i'd left off
it dawned on me
Dan had never stopped eating
during the whole mess
wiping his mouth
he took a gulp of java
pulled out a cigarette
asked the waitress
for a book of matches
looked at me as if he'd
missed it all
took a long drag
from his Marlboro
saw how much food
was still on my plate
exhaled a casual
cloud of smoke
held out his
empty cup
for a refill

race war

"yeah," he said, "guys at work are buying
guns and shit...storing 'em in the desert
for the big race war."

immediately i begin to regret
the many times i refused to go
hunting with my stepfather
never acquiring the taste for
blood and guts, the violent
scattering of feathers in mid air
or the nonsensical pumping of shells
into a ball of fur.

taking a sip from my wine cooler,
i study him...an aryan bull.
i imagine him and myself
locked in hand to hand combat,
a classic battle.
but i know that's not how it will be,
because a scared man is a crazy one.

it will come from behind, and i won't even know
what hit me.

California, here i go

approaching the border at Needles
i feel the crosshairs being lifted
from my back
this land where i was born
of beaches and brazen bikinis
coppertone and year round makeout
sessions at the local drive-in
the minor inconvenience of 5 a.m.
wakeup calls while the crust beneath
our beds shifted an inch...or two
this land that i truly felt was paradise on earth
(once i actually asked a nun why Adam
and Eve left in the first place,
surely they could have settled in Boyle
Heights, maybe even owned a liquor store)
the haze of sweet smoke as we sat
with our legs crossed
puffing on pipe bowls of thai stick or
red hair sensemian, flushing our brains out
with the communal bottle of Cuervo 1800
this land where our real homes
are our cars
as we snake through valleys named
after spanish saints and dodge bullets
when we forget to use our turn signals
this land where dreams are devoured
like the body of Christ

this land where white fingers point
at their brown dishwashers, gardeners, cooks,
nannies, garbage collectors, ditch diggers,
the same people whose sweat is the oil
lubricating the machine so the rest of us can
sliiiiiiiiide....

crossing into Arizona, i look in
the rearview mirror, take in one last sunset
feel the crosshairs lifted
from my back
sigh in relief
begin to cry

waiting in line at Logli's...Rockford, IL.

oh Logli...oh Logli
your checkstands manned by the brides
of blue collar workers
these women who move with the
urgency of junkies high on opium
they make the loathesome lines at the
dept. of motor vehicles
look like an "E" ticket ride
at Disneyland

as i pile my groceries up
on her one square foot of
counter space
my Logli girl intently reads
the recipe for "pork chops surprise"
on the back of my can of
cream of mushroom soup
her lanquid Logli eyes
speak to me of brats and beer on hot humid
weekends, her cheeks flush with excitement
only when her favorite NASCAR driver
slams another into the wall

is it this
just this

as her Logli breasts sigh
rise and fall like soft loaves of
fresh baked sourdough
i smother myself in dreams of
tractor pulls and this
slow-so-slow pace
here in this midwest

this holy place
this life
this Logli

turning into strangers

under the cover
of early morning darkness
i lay on my side
silently watch her gray
outline rise and fall
with the soothing
sounds of her breathing
can smell the stale love
and despair clinging
to the sheets
like last night's
cigarette smoke

a few hours later
the car packed
i give her my key
step outside where
the cold air of a
midwest February
slaps me in the face

the glowing embers
between us
once bright
now cold ashes
scattered on the winds
of this endless winter

divorce me

she says
her resolve gone
having waited a year
for me to come
to my senses

i can see the danger
in her eyes
because the holidays
are upon us now
that time when people
sit down to eat with
the perfect strangers
collectively called "family"
when empty liquor bottles take
up more and more space
in the local landfills

when loneliness and dread
knock on our door
in the middle of the night
hand us a loaded gun
console us
like the compassionate
neighbors we no longer have

divorce me
she says
pained and hurt
while in the corner of the room
the Christmas decorations
wait to be unpacked

little booby traps
set to explode
in our hands

karma

i was a cockroach
once
in another life

i learned to live
in any environment
the cool damp spot
under a cretaceous rock
a crack in the crystalized
dirt floor of an atom
bomb test site
didn't mind the lack of light
did most of my fun stuff
in the dark anyway
learned to relish the flesh
of my own kind in a pinch
but through the ages developed
a diverse set of tastebuds

survived famine flood
fire plague and
the ghostly trace of t.v. radiation
beamed from the Home Shopping
Network at 3 a.m. on a Saturday
adapted to ultrasound waves
"super-duper-intensified-guaranteed-
to-kill-me" bug spray and
attractive roach condos
complete with complimentary open bar
suspiciously tainted
happy hour food

would lick the potato chip grease
off your fingers and
daringly nibble
the chunks of steak

stuck between
your teeth when you
fell asleep
with your mouth
open

i was one hell of a cockroach
made sure my DNA
would be carried in a trillion
offspring
had the routine down pat

then i died
came back
a human being

her first porno

she was watching
her first porno video
so we dropped by for
moral support
it was John Wayne Bobbitt's
version of what happened
on the fateful night
his mrs. decided to
cut to the root of
their marital problems

we couldn't last
the whole thing
the little limp
dick with a 90 degree
bend where it had
been miraculously
reattached
brought to mind
a baby mud turtle
sunning itself on
a rock
we were laughing
so hard our sides
hurt

so when the
vcr was turned off
we found ourselves
watching the Three
Stooges and the
inevitable came to mind
Moe, Larry, and Curly
in a porno film
Moe picking up
a hammer and saying

"a couple of wise guys, eh?"
and pounding little heads
into submission
or the big
pie throwing scene
bodies covered with
whipped cream
Curly diving in
grinning while licking
some matron's big fat butt
until he realizes the
moaning he is hearing
sounds a lot like Moe
and while he is getting
poked in the eyes
the coppers knock down
the door busting everyone
except the Stooges

who jump through a window
escape running down
the street
weenies flapping in the breeze
like three blind mice

"Okla. bombing remains to be buried...

More than four years after the Oklahoma City bombing, unidentified, fragmentary remains will be buried in a memorial grove of trees at the state Capitol... All 168 victims of the April 19, 1995, bombing that destroyed the Alfred P. Murrah Federal Building were identified, but these small bits of tissue and bone could not be linked to any specific body... " Rockford Register Star - 11/23/99

today the wind swoops
down from a grey sky
blows cold across the river
kicks up the last
of the fallen leaves
the bare branches
of the trees shake
and vibrate like
the bones of the dead

i gather my collection
scales of dried skin
fingernail clippings
strands of my hair
prick myself and milk
my blood
drop by drop
wrap it all
in a white handkerchief
bury it in a hole
by the Rock River
dug with my bare hands
i mix salt in the dirt
so nothing will
ever grow there again
pack the soft clay
with the heel of my boot

i refuse to mark
your death with a tree
a garden or a statue
but instead with this
barren spot of earth
desolate and sterile
a personal tribute

let those of the future
walk by this odd memorial
ponder this lifeless patch
of soil surrounded by
so much life

eventually
someone will say
"it doesn't make sense"
and each time those words
are spoken or thought
one more scream clinging
to the inner walls of
our collective mind
will become silent

until all that remains
is the ringing in our ears

"... I am God."

and why not?
i put cruelty in nature
for a purpose
the lion's face
lathered in red glistening
saliva like a death mask
while gorging
on its prey or the fight
of desperation a
moth makes
as it struggles in a web
jeweled with morning
dew are all part
of my master plan

but you...
your crude attempts to
outdo me everytime
i doze off have finally
rubbed me the wrong way

even i know fear when
looking into the eyes of men
seeing the icy knives
waiting to thrust and cut
i search for a place to puke
while watching the helpless
slaughtered with the cold
calculation of an algebraic equation;
poor+powerless=expendable squared

i've been a hands off
deity long enough
neglecting you like
a single parent working
two full-time jobs

well, not anymore
now i walk among you
and i'm taking you down
one at a time

survival

my California friends send me pictures
of their new homes in the republican hills
of Orange County
a place where they named the airport
after John Wayne

they tell me things over the phone like:
trading the BMW for a vintage jag
a steal from another desperate sucker
going down for the count
the deep sea fishing in Cabo San Lucas
is better than ever   cheaper too
thanks to another plunge by the peso
now that they have a wine cellar
the search is on for the perfect chardonnay
meaning frequent trips to Santa Barbara and beyond
the business sold for big big bucks
and damn the dilemma of what to do
after an early retirement

i want to send them pictures of my new place
poetry books stacked around an army
sleeping bag on the floor
in a room a little larger than O.J.'s jail cell

my response:
a six pack of coronas is the closest
i'll be getting to the border for quite awhile
my 10 yr. old Nissan leaks like the car
Sonny Corleone was driving when they
were both turned into a piece of swiss cheese
i live in a town where public reaction to
Madonna's latest movie makes front page news
and yes
it's snowing   again
i want to cry out
i'm so cold
so alone

but i don't
because not long ago i stood there with them
jostling for my space on the 405 freeway
the perfect tan really meant something
mimosa brunches with cheap caviar
and views of blonde surfers bobbing in
the white foam   the girls golden brown with
skin so tight and smooth a quarter would bounce
10 inches off their firm butt cheeks

but the miles between us
have changed the view
from here
my friends look like lemmings
little fucking lemmings
drawn to the sea

who never see the approaching fall
until just before their brains
go splat

on the rocks below

to an Iraqi poet

while i am shown
generals on CNN
doing comic shtick
to the video images
sent back from weapons
smarter than them
they would have me believe
you have jars of mustard
gas fermenting in your cellar
petri dishes of black jello
ripening in your fridge
you are the crazed islamic
warrior turning armageddon
into something more than
just another computer game
achieving spiritual completion
only when the fires of mass
destruction lick the eyebrows
off our faces

i will not be shown your grief
as you sift through the rubble
of our drive-by missile strikes
pulling out the limp bodies of
your crushed and bloodied babies
i will not be shown the women
crying at the funerals of their
husbands and sons as they implore
Allah to retaliate without mercy
on this land of coca cola and
super bowl Sundays

you and i
could change all this
meet at some clandestine
location and build a missile
of words
launch it into the bureaucratic
bellies of our leaders

who bring me shame
and you, pain

then
we could hold hands
bow our heads
cleanse ourselves with
our tears
pray in a language
we would both
understand

Godzilla

he was a big schlep
half dinosaur/half rubberized foam
but they needed to give
the real monster we had
unleashed on them a form
easy to understand,
powers that made sense
(the way his radiation-
glow-green-breath leveled
the city as his roar sounded
like one of those horns
God's chosen people would
blow to knock down the
walls of their enemies)

of course we bastardized
the original, softened
the images of the burnt
and vaporized
instead gave ourselves
Raymond Burr smudged
with dirt and a bandage
around his head while
he played the poster boy pipe
smoking american observer
a presbyterian Hugh Hefner
surrounded by foreign
hysteria and chaos
but never forget
we made Godzilla
gave him the power
to destroy and resurrect
so when he comes for us
appears off the shores of
San Diego or New York
returning like our prodigal son

expecting to be welcomed
with open arms
we will have no one
to blame but ourselves
and justice will be served

5/16/02

8 months later

i served during peacetime
never had to take the point
on a real patrol

but now i know what it's like
to see every crack in the
sidewalk

to study strangers approaching me
from afar and gauge how close
is close enough

i hear barking dogs 3 blocks away
and ask why

in public places i sit facing the door
anticipate the look that says
"i-don't-have-anything-to-lose"
the icy gaze raising up to God
just before the unleashing of hell
on earth

at night i dream
of silver pterodactyls
blinded by the sun
circling for a place
to land

and angels
angels falling from the sky
with singed wings

Van Gogh's ear

found it in the gutter
downtown Chicago
picked it up
put it in my pocket
now it goes everywhere i go
never leave home without it

the FBI found out
invited me to a
mandatory interview
they consider Vincent subversive
a terrorist of art
but a terrorist
just the same
they gave me crayons
blank paper
told me to draw something
i colored red white & blue
planes dropping bombs & food
on poor people
they were convinced
i was a-ok

today i held it close
to my own ear
wanted to hear
what it hears

i listened for a long time
the silence almost
drove me crazy

what love is... for A.C.

i need this turmoil
this wild mushroom woman
who stirs up the settled
dust of my life
i need this whirling dervish diva
singing jazz under black
silk nights and dead stars
i need her estrogen sparks
to balance out my moody
testosterone tirades

i need to plug
into this dancing goddess
feel her charge my
mad poetman juices
i need her sharp teeth
biting into my sirloin steak soul
watch red blood drip
from the corner of her mouth
i need to lay next to
this living landscape
booby trapped with
abandoned mine fields
pitted with the scars
of loves past

i need war and peace
holy visions and raging nightmares
i need her to want me
to despise me
pull me close
push me away

the man was right, love is a
dog from hell, so take it from one
more son of a bitch who knows

once you've had it
like this
you don't want it
any other way

how it was

imagine you are in a car race
one of those european grand prixs
where they go for 24 hrs. straight
1/2 way through something happens
you sneeze you nod
for just a second
close your eyes at the worst
possible time
then the car is spinning
the centrifugal force pulling
your eyeballs out of their sockets
then rolling into the wall
at 150 mph. and death is
on top of you slipping her tongue
down your throat
the flames licking your suit
ignite a natural reaction
muscles push pull lift
you out and while leaping
through mid air taking a look
over your shoulder at a wall
of flame brighter than a cop's
flashlight in your face at midnight
you can hear the blisters forming
on the bottoms of your feet
ssssssssssssssssssss..............
you hit the ground flat
on your chest   pop up
sprint the fastest 100 yd. dash
ever by a two legged animal
and while running give thanks
to the god who had the sense to
create survival instincts

that's
how it was

the day
i left you

my brother-in-law calls to say...

two days away from a double bypass
he calls to talk football and discuss
what a wild season it's been so far
teams that didn't have a chance last year
now undefeated and you just can't
predict anymore
changing the subject i ask him
if he's scared and he says yes
trying to lighten the mood i tell him
to mark all his body parts with funny
remarks like "don't cut here"
"don't even think about it"
"i'm having heart surgery, stupid"
because i saw Oprah's show about
hospital horror stories
i also want to tell him
surgery should never be
scheduled for the end of the week
but it's too late for that
(remembering the night we caught
him outside my sister's window
my stepfather unleashed me
like one of his prized hunting dogs
i gave chase over to the next block
found him hiding behind some bushes
and while he tried to talk his way out
i made sure my punch came from
the same fist wearing my class ring
for maximum damage)

but over the years he proved
us wrong about his
loyalty and devotion
sticking by my sister's side
as she wrestled free from

dark family secrets and the
madness of our past

he showed me how a man
forgives and forgets
always greeting me with
a smile and a cold beer
never a hint of bitterness
in his handshake

now he's making calls
to the people he cares about
i'm honored to be
on the list as we make
small talk shadowed
in the understanding of what
could go wrong
both of us refusing
to bring it up

yes, Anthony
it is a topsy turvy season
the ball bouncing in strange and
mysterious ways
but may the angels huddle over you
as your gentle heart is exposed to the world

and
may the flame of compassion
burn bright in your chest
for many super bowls
to come

for the woman who cuts my hair

i watch in the mirror
a tiny sparrow hopping from
one side of my nest
to the other
she selects and snips
by instinct
leaving no unruly lock
unturned

been with her for three years
the one relationship i haven't
managed to screw up
realizing it's a good thing
to have at least one woman in my life
i can trust within three feet of me
as she holds a sharp pointed object
in her hands

almost blew it
between appointments i took
a pair of scissors to my annoying bangs
gave myself a little trim
our next time together
she was icy as a scorned lover
acted like she found lipstick on my collar
her suspicions eased only when i 'fessed up
promised not to do it again

she cares about me too
disapproves of my alley cat lifestyle
offers unsolicited advice on behalf
of her many sisters
nudges me to settle down
and get soft around the edges

when i feel sorry for myself
wonder if the relationship fairy
has crossed me off her list
i imagine Carla sitting in her chair
cleaning the implements of her trade
biding her time

until i walk through her door
predictable and consistent
loyal and faithful
coming back like
she knew i would
coming back for more

altar... for Kathy

like an old non-practicing catholic
who can't give up the rituals
i light sacred candles on my window ledge
improvise prayers whispered to the wind
hope somehow they will find their way to you

the green candle is for the time we stayed up
throughout the night revealing how pain and loneliness
have been our closest companions since who knew when
made us lean and strong in spirit
able to remain distant in crowds
provided the shield we needed to go through life unscathed
realizing we belonged to the same wandering tribe
you took my hand and placed it on your small
delicate breast
said you wanted me to touch you
our defenses dropped almost as quickly
as the clothes hitting the floor
around our happy feet

the blue candle is the purr lodged in your throat
when i would come from behind
plant my kiss between your shoulder blades
slide my thumbs under the elastic of your panties
and slowly pull down while my tongue left
a slow sticky trail along your spine
an amourous snail looking for your sex
one lick at a time

when i light the red one...
ahh, the red one
i see the first night you got up from our bed
tiptoed to the closet and returned with your
black leather belt
begged me to use it
whispered in my ear the thing you wanted me to do

scared but curious i lashed out at your pure unblemished ass
felt the heat of your desire scorch my lips
as i kissed the rising welts crisscrossing your flushed bottom

and this candle
this candle is the day i walked out your door
it was November then
it has been November ever since
other women proving to me (as you knew they would)
it doesn't get any better than what i had with you
now, even during summer's hottest day when heat
rises from blacktop
blurry and rippled with a life of its own
i am cold and barren inside

my heart
a tree
which has lost
all its leaves

McLife II

sitting here
eating a couple of
fish sandwiches
imagining a sleepy eyed clown
by the edge of a lake
his line breaking the glassy surface
at sunrise
but it is most likely
a european fishing fleet using those
new fangled nets that drift
with the currents and kill
all fish big and small
i'm feeling guilty now
but not enough to stop eating
arriving like clockwork
the single parents towing
kids behind line them up
looking like the birds on early summer
mornings combing the lawns
blackholes wide
chirp chirp chirp chirp
stuffing happy meals down tiny throats
happy parent happy kid happy plastic toy
made in a third world country
by a kid younger than the one
now playing with it
driving daddy's new red buick
three teenage babes walk in dressed
in blue collar chic
through the smell of hot grease
and burning meat i sniff the deodorant
they use
the scent of the perfume they got for christmas
the fruity sweet lip gloss on their
full pink lips
the soap they showered in this morning

an old woman who could be
their grandmother is working
cleaning the windows
this old woman who once had
a great pair of gams and danced
to devil music by cats named Basie,
Duke, and Miller as she
fought off the octopus
hands of her drunk dates
sweaty and stinking of beer and smoke

the black kids arriving at the
start of their shift
frying the fries
flipping the patties
spreading the buns
making an honest dollar
trying to make it to their
eighteenth birthday

this is where America eats
where we fill our bellies
and stuff our cheeks
here here here
at McDonald's
the feeding trough
of this all consuming
nation

Walton's girls

i always thought it would be Erin
the saucy redhead with the farm girl charm
and those wide curvaceous hips just made for
popping out another double digit brood

when doing the mundane chores that must be done
so the family farm could survive i would fantasize
about the two of us in the backseat of her old man's car
parked on some secluded Virginia backroad while
her shapely white calves wrapped themselves around me
and bounced off my backside as i would play connect-the-dots
with her freckles and my tongue, and i dare say those freckles
were everywhere

so you can imagine my surprise when instead
it was the older one, Mary Ellen who came to me
this angel of mercy who was tough enough
to make me stand up straight, get a haircut,
make something of myself
she is a wrestler, always putting up a fight
until she's ready, and then she gives of herself
like the passionate madonna that she is
she strokes my ego by moaning at just the right moments
and she can twist off the cap on a beer bottle with her tongue

but lately, when we go to the big house for Sunday dinner
Erin sits across the table from me, and halfway through the meal
she has begun to slowly slide her bare foot
up my leg
and i don't know what to do

for Emily, my waitress at the Irish Rose

who
floats through the room
soft as a cloud of smoke
from a french cigarette
juggles glasses of house merlot
with mystical grace
this bad girl angel
in leather studded collar
comes to me in fishnet dreams
gives me glimpses of billowy
cleavage while she hovers
over my table
her red chili pepper lips glisten
in the soft light of the room
as recorded jazz
starts her round hips to slowly
shift left then roll right
the wiggle in her walk
makes me forget what
i'm supposed to be eating
then she comes close
leans down
her sultry voice whispering
in my ear
"tip me...
tip...
me...
big..."

i'm a ruined man
as my wallet
spreads open
quicker and wider
than the parting
of the Red Sea

leaving Rockford

it happened without warning
one day i woke up
sniffed the scent of decay
felt a cold damp worm
burrowing into my bones
watched my poems
fall to the ground
dried up and lifeless

loaded my belongings
into the back of a u-haul
left at dusk like an NFL owner
sneaking out of town
headed for the interstate
caught the nearest on ramp
submitted to the magnetic pull
between earth and moon
studied the stars like a
AAA road map

finally understood how
Cortes felt the day he
torched his ships
watched them sink
into the sea

then marched desperate
and blind towards
the new world
with nothing left
to lose

godfather

make no mistake
the first time i held you
just home from the hospital
breath smelling sweet and sour
wrapped up like a little mummy
your tiny head resting on my shoulder
that first time you turned
and gently nudged my neck
with your little puppy nose
giving me a sloppy kiss
that first time
i knew i would
live or die for you
it didn't matter which
i just knew

now i watch from afar
worry about the lessons
you've yet to learn
the nights you'll cry
yourself asleep
envision the hearts you'll break
the prices you'll pay
the promises waiting to be broken
or kept

always remember this
my lovelies
i'm the godfather
the nino
your ace in the hole
the man in the background
the one they
wouldn't recognize
approaching in
a dark alley until

it's too late
or just another face
shaking their hand
on your wedding day

i'm the godfather
bonded for life
sworn to be faithful
and loyal no matter
what you do

never seen
but always there

Genesis... Beatty Park

walking home from work
after two days of snow
the street lights were
on because it was dark
and up ahead by the park

with the sacred indian mounds
under the artificial light
the wind had created a
swirling cloud of snow dust
icy electrons circling
in the chaos of creation

knowing an epiphany
when i see one
i approached it
marveled at the work
of a pure artist
stood there in the midst
of infant stars
and the birth
of another cosmos

Mars outside my window

at first it was something special
hadn't been seen this close
since my ancestors wrapped
themselves with animal skins
and picking someone's lice
was a sign of affection

i'd wake up at three a.m.
stick my head outside
find it in the early morning sky
wonder what celestial cause
and effect awaited me

i soon found out
lost my job
got deeper in debt
as i shot resumes into
the black void like
flares from a desperate man
praying to be found

unemployed
almost three months later
it's still out there
dim but persistent
i wake up
look out my window
shake my head

whisper "goddamn"
to no one
in particular

4 eyes

used to be i could take them
or leave them but now they
are a necessity
i have to know where they
are at all times
spontaneity is out
now when i want to
read in the bathroom
it's an event
i have to plan
and prepare

map reading and menus
have become two of the most
difficult things i do
without my spectacles
i act like i know where
i'm going
order the blue plate special
when i get there
throw my fate to the winds
and try not to act surprised

the proximity required
during sex has turned
me into a lascivious little
mole squinting my way
from moan to musky moan
faulty peepers giving
my lover all the visual detail
found in Monet's last painting

can still see objects from afar
just not when they
are going to hit me in the face

which
depending on your
point of view
isn't necessarily
a bad thing

McLife III

i'm sitting in the corner
eating my Big Mac and reading the paper
when some of the old people
from the senior citizen rest home
across the street start to arrive
for after dinner coffee and conversation
the workers know all of them
on a first name basis
even let them carry in their own dessert
they talk about who was taken
to the hospital and who just got back
death isn't mentioned but is just around
the corner like that burger pushing clown
whose picture hangs in the lobby
then this one little silver headed lady
in her best polyester pant suit
her rouge colored cheekbones
making her look like
the grim reaper in drag
jumps up and starts to do the charleston
she dances up to the counter
the people standing in line smile and clap
she dances for the cop drinking a coke
and doing his paperwork
she dances for the guy sitting alone
and talking to himself
she dances for all of us
until she sits back down
her tiny heart clinching
like a tight fist in her chest
daring someone
anyone to show her
that goddamned light
we're all supposed to see
near the end

after awhile
she gets up
crosses the street
chalks up one more day

Ricardo, janitor of the U.S.S. Enterprise

nobody knows i exist
but who do you think keeps those
squeaky clean hallways looking like that?
and everytime our pendejo of a captain
navigates us right into the local magnetic-gravitational-
time-warp-space-flux-super-duper-ever-ready-force-field
and half the crew upchucks their breakfast, who puts in
the double shift?
sure, every ship needs guys like me to do the dirty work
but there's no need for the recruiters to lie about there being
plenty of room for advancement
i'm not blind, i know the only way we can
get into the academy is by landing jobs in the kitchen
so here i am, and let me tell you, it never ceases to amaze me
how people can get so dumb the more important they become
take the captain, for instance
one thing for sure, this cabron will never suffer from a prolonged
case of blue balls...the dude boinks anything in skirts,
and gets away with it!
i thought it was the v-waist figure he gets from wearing that
girdle all the time, but when i mail ordered mine and wore it
for a week, nobody noticed, even when i had to mop standing
straight up cause the chingon wouldn't let me bend at the waist
everyone knows he always goes on those landing parties
(why do you think they call them that?) because he's constantly
looking for some strange action
rumor has it, and i find this one hard to believe,
during one of these excursions the old man
actually found time to get laid by a green chick...
talk about thinking with your chorizo! all i know is
he kept a daily appointment with the doc for two straight weeks

well, last week i was up for promotion
and as i stood at attention in front of his desk
in my best uniform, hair brushed, shoes shined, brass polished
he told me what a great job i was doing

a clean ship is a godly ship, my contribution to the morale
of the crew was priceless...i had so much bullshit packed up my ass
i thought i was gonna explode
then he said he couldn't promote me at this time
because i didn't take the initiative to enroll in a leadership course
being offered on the ship and i needed to work on my
physical appearance, maybe do daily sit ups and pass on
the free tacos during happy hour at the enlisted club
when i thought of how i spent Christmas Eve cleaning up
after the officer's party and how the stink of vulcan vomit
lingered with me for days no matter how many showers i took...
well, it just didn't seem right

today, while cleaning the captain's quarters
i found his supply of condoms, and without hesitation
i pulled out my trusty micro-laser swedish army knife
and proceeded to make minute punctures in every one

like my great ancestor Juan Luis Enrique Hidalgo Dolores
Garcia Vargas said as he was climbing the walls of the Alamo
"fuck 'em if they can't take a joke."

hard peepees...

In that dizzy moment/did your peepee dangle/like a ripcord,
or is it true all men/have hard-ons/when they fall to earth?

"Jumping off Roofs"—**Sandra Cisneros**

I

i too, jumped from roofs and eventually out of a plane
for me it was like being born again
leaving a perfectly good place
leaping into who-knows-what
i forgot to pray those four seconds when i was suspended 1700 ft. in the air
like a seed looking for a place to land
my chute yanked me with a jerk as it caught the wind
and yes, Sandra, my peepee was hard

II

i was only four standing on the front seat of my old man's
car as we took a ride to visit my nana and on the way we passed
a woman walking on the sidewalk wearing a tight dress
her hips swayed back and forth like she'd been watching way too many
Barbara Stanwyck movies
i remember the boiling in my little belly all warm and nice
the rough material of my Sears and Roebuck blue jeans rubbing against
my nub of a penis when i said,
"daddy, when i see a pretty lady my peepee gets hard"
he laughed so loud i thought he was gonna crash

III

this bully who had been held back two or three times was extorting money
from us during lunch
we would carry our brown bags to the picnic tables like paranoid gazelles
looking for the awaiting pounce and flash of teeth
when it was my turn i wanted to fork over the coin but my peepee said no
as we rolled on the ground i drew first blood and all his previous victims
surrounded us cheered me on and the blows to his face got harder and meaner
until a teacher broke it up and escorted us to the principal's office
i noticed a girl looking at me her cheeks blushing red like roses
my defiant erection sending the message i was not to be fucked with anymore

IV
Sandra, i believe a hard peepee is a state of mind
which means i have been that way ninety-eight percent of my life
while some of us dangle like yo-yos on a string
there are those of us who walk this earth proudly pointing towards the sky
where we belong
where the angels
patiently await our return

Richard Vargas was born and raised in Los Angeles and Orange Counties, where he attended California State University, Long Beach. From 1977-80 he published and edited five issues of *The Tequila Review*. He was stationed at Ft. Carson, Colorado, lived in Rockford, IL., and is currently residing in Albuquerque, NM.

Readers may contact the author at: picodegallo54@yahoo.com